Chaplain Handbook

A Devotional Guide for Trail Life Chaplains

John Burkitt

with

Bill Goins

&

Parson's Porch Books

www.parsonsporchbooks.com

Chaplain Handbook: A Devotional Guide for Trail Life Chaplains

ISBN: Softcover 978-1-951472-44-3

To Richard John Mathews

(1957-2020)

Strong Family Man,

Devoted Christian,

Child Welfare Advocate,

True Friend

Welcome, Chaplain!

Welcome, Chaplain! You are part of a ministry of ordained and laypeople that have proudly wear the Trail Life uniform. You will share your faith with youth and adults at Troop meetings and outings, but you will also:

- ***Model*** Christ's love and wisdom.
- ***Provide*** counselling, oversight and encouragement.
- ***Interpret*** nature as a testament to God's power and goodness.

That's a big job, yet remember God does not call the equipped, he equips the called. Your willingness to serve is your greatest qualification. Your willingness to learn is your second greatest. You will have support from your fellow Troop and Area leaders, an opportunity for in-person training, and this Handbook. These resources will take you from where you are to where you want to be, preparing you for the unique challenges and opportunities of outdoor ministry, and outlining how Trail Life addresses the challenges facing our youth.

Be sure to always wear the Trail Life Troop uniform. It will serve you well unadorned or accessorized with your clerical sash or collar. When you first put it on, you will feel a surge of pride, walking a little straighter and taller, and for good reason. That distinctive uniform is the green of meadow and woodland, the visible badge of your Trail Life family, the full armor of God, and a sign to the community and yourself that you believe in the potential of your fellow Trailmen, are willing to stretch yourself beyond your comfort zone with patience, humility and humor. It is a mark of your intent to Walk Worthy.

In His Service,

John Burkitt

Contents

A Trailman Honors God

Trail Life USA is not just an outdoor program with a ministry, it's a ministry with exciting outdoor adventure that glorifies God as it edifies Trailmen. Every Trail Life troop is chartered to a religious organization that subscribes to our Statement of Faith and Values and considers us an integral part of their mission. Seen in that light, your job is clearly a forethought, not an afterthought.

While our stance on Christianity is non-sectarian, our faith does have definite shape and substance. It embraces a traditional reading of scripture, giving young men new life rather than new doctrine. All adult leaders from the dad who drives the van to our Home Office staff must agree to our Statement of Faith and Values. While youth members need not affirm the Christian religion, the environment they inhabit, the instruction they receive, and the code of conduct they follow will all glorify Christ as the only begotten Son of God, the savior of the world.

When you initiate a Troop or Patrol prayer, it is customary to doff your hat and say, "A Trailman Honors God." This honor It is not merely something Trailmen do, it's what that makes them Trailmen. The nature of that honor is spelled out in our Statement of Faith and Values, as well as our Mission and Motto:

STATEMENT OF FAITH:

We believe there is One Triune God – God the Father; Jesus Christ, His one and only Son; and the Holy Spirit – Creator of the universe and eternally existent. We believe the Holy Scriptures

(Old and New Testaments) to be the inspired and authoritative Word of God. We believe each person is created in His image for the purpose of communing with and worshiping God. We believe in the ministry of the Holy Spirit, who enables us to live godly lives. We believe each of us is called to love the Lord our God with all our heart, mind, soul, and strength, and to love our neighbors as ourselves. We believe God calls us to lives of purity, service, stewardship and integrity.

STATEMENT OF VALUES:

Purity: *God calls us to lives of holiness, being pure of heart, mind, word and deed. We are to reserve sexual activity for the sanctity of marriage, a lifelong commitment before God between a man and a woman.*

Service: *God calls us to become responsible members of our community and the world through selfless acts that contribute to the welfare of others.*

Stewardship: *God calls us to use our God-given time, talents, and money wisely.*

Integrity: *God calls us to live moral lives that demonstrate an inward motivation to do what is biblically right regardless of the cost.*

MISSION STATEMENT

Our Mission is to guide generations of courageous young men to honor God, lead with integrity, serve others, and experience outdoor adventure.

MOTTO

Walk Worthy!

A ministry that stands for nothing will fall for anything. To protect our cherished values, we carefully defined certain beliefs and principles which bring unity from the diversity of Trail Life:

- Our Christianity is the traditional, Trinitarian understanding of the Old and New Testaments. *"In the beginning was the Word, and the Word was with God." - John 1:1.*

- Our Troops may approach Christianity from the Catholic, Orthodox, Protestant or Nondenominational viewpoint. Our official documents are all non-sectarian.
- Our faith is consistent with the historic Nicene Creed.

THE NICENE CREED

I believe in one God, the Father almighty, maker of heaven and earth, of all things visible and invisible.

I believe in one Lord Jesus Christ, the Only Begotten Son of God, born of the Father before all ages. God from God, Light from Light, true God from true God, begotten, not made, consubstantial with the Father; through him all things were made.

For us men and for our salvation he came down from heaven, and by the Holy Spirit was incarnate of the Virgin Mary and became man.

For our sake he was crucified under Pontius Pilate, he suffered death and was buried, and rose again on the third day in accordance with the Scriptures. He ascended into heaven and is seated at the right hand of the Father. He will come again in glory to judge the living and the dead and his kingdom will have no end.

I believe in the Holy Spirit, the Lord, the giver of life, who proceeds from the Father and the Son, who with the Father and the Son is adored and glorified, who has spoken through the prophets.

I believe in one, holy, catholic and apostolic Church. I confess one Baptism for the forgiveness of sins, and I look forward to the resurrection of the dead and the life of the world to come. Amen.*

(Universal)*

To us, faith is not an opinion, a belief, or a philosophy

In modern culture, faith is often equated with an opinion, a belief or at best a philosophy. If your "faith" fits these criteria, you will get along just fine in popular culture.

- You can hold the ***opinion*** that God exists. Yet His position is not an elected one. You cannot be saved by your favorite color, or by simply conceding the existence of God.

- You can ***believe*** the Bible is the Word of God. So does Satan, for all the good it will do him. I believe in penguins, but frankly they haven't changed me in the least.
- You can have a ***philosophy*** such as, "A sucker is born every minute," which seeks to explain something or influence you, but does not require a response. "A penny saved is a penny earned," saves money, not souls. Principles are fine but so are tools—both must be used in order to be useful.

A moment's reflection will assure you no Christian ever died in the Coliseum for an opinion, a belief, or a philosophy. If—God forbid—you should ever have to face the lions, do it for something worth dying for! Faith is a gift from God that leads you to live a transformed life. It is nothing less than a call to action. It is precisely this action that will run afoul of popular culture and its sensibilities.

Christ encountered Scribes, Pharisees and Sadducees that held radically different opinions, beliefs, and philosophies. Nevertheless, these three bitterly opposed groups worshipped and sacrificed together. They had a cultural truce that allowed them to coexist by considering religious beliefs a matter of purely personal concern. Matthew 16:24 records that, "Then Jesus told his disciples, *If anyone would come after me, let him deny himself and take up his cross and follow me*." Christ was not looking for an inoffensive motto that would fly under the radar. The Great Commission respects and implies peace with justice, yet it does not excuse you from proclaiming the good news of the Gospel and working toward that day when every knee shall bow, and every tongue confess that Jesus is Lord.

Trail Life does not put faith in its own box; faith gets applied to choices to build character, and faith gets applied to life to develop fitness. The promotion of character and fitness is therefore an integral part of shepherding faith. The four elements of character; self-respect, self-control, self-worth and self-reliance, are vital parts of expressing faith in choices. The four elements of fitness; physical, mental, emotional and moral, are vital parts of expressing faith in a lifestyle.

Last but not least, there are people in Trail Life praying for you. If you have the least doubt about your qualifications, have confidence in their prayers and in the God that assures us He answers them. Now go forth and "Walk Worthy!"

Outdoor Adventure

Among youth development programs and ministries, Trail Life stands out in the degree to which its ministry and outdoor adventure aspects are integrated at every level. This was by design.

So why conduct a ministry within the matrix of outdoor adventure? Step outside your four walls and look around you! Even in your suburban environment, the song of birds breaks in on you the way God, with a baby's cry, broke in on the world. God's creation has abundant, unchanging values of beauty and truth, equally relevant to each new generation. Come to the woodlands and let their gentle wisdom into your heart. Nature involves the mind, heart, soul and body. It expands horizons and inspires wonder. As Rudyard Kipling put it:

Who hath smelt wood-smoke at twilight?
Who hath heard the birch-log burning?
Who is quick to read the noises of the night?

Let him follow with the others,
For the Young Men's feet are turning
To the camps of proved desire and known delight!

Day by day we surround ourselves with the works of our own hands and listen to the stories we tell ourselves about life. Find the courage to step away for a time into the works of God's hands and you are soon surrounded by His eternal truths. There you remember that you too are the work of God's hands, and that His hands will lift you when you stumble. That is the Trail of Trail Life, a literal and figurative journey from where you are to where you need to be.

Nature gracefully sidesteps the technology barrier that inhibits inter-generational sharing in modern culture. The time-honored heritage of fathers and grandfathers is received by the young men whose hearts burn like the campfire and whose eyes shine like the stars.

Nature simplifies and clarifies. In its classroom we can learn essential things about ourselves, others, and God. And one of the greatest things we learn is that Nature, like the Body of Christ, is made up of many diverse things which yet work together. Predator and prey in their breathless dance keep their drama well-rehearsed. Warm moist winds caress cool currents and nature weeps with rustic joy. Sun and moon mark the passage of hours and seasons. Stars lend a helping hand to the travelers of the night. Woodland boughs and desert dunes both have their unique allure, celebrating the diversity within God's universal truths.

You don't have to superimpose God on nature, something akin to jabbing a carrot into a chocolate cake where it will remain uneaten. Trail Life seeks to reveal God in everything, with the Christian lifestyle contributing to the program the way carrots add to carrot cake. Christianity is inherent to Trail Life and an inseparable part of walking worthy.

With so much glorious forethought, we avoid blatantly "Godding" the program with afterthoughts. The program, done right, celebrates the love and grace of Jesus Christ with effortless joy. Unlike things made by man, the lovely and challenging things wrought by God can speak for themselves. Your job is to get people to pay attention.

We appreciate what we understand and incorporate what we appreciate. If your young men are led to understand Christ in his wilderness, they will come to invite Him in.

Christian Character

While we can't ***appease*** God, we can yet ***please*** God, and while character may not ***save*** the world, it still ***serves*** the world. Our mission is to guide young men to have courage, honor God, lead with integrity and serve others.

They don't do those things solely to die in righteousness, they also do them to live righteously, modelling Christ. They do these things because they see a role for their obedience and sacrifice in, "Thy Kingdom come, Thy Will be done on earth as it is in heaven."

Human is ***what*** we are, and character is ***who*** we are. Our character, which is to say our unique personhood, is built through experience, which is why the experiences you choose to have are important. We give you plenty of great opportunities to choose from along the Trail. You may be one of those chaplains who comes out to camp for an hour on Sunday mornings. You may be one who is champing at the bit for each outdoor experience and is the first one to grab a canoe paddle or a walking stick. Either way, that's okay, but keep in mind that you and your fellow adult leaders are approaching the same goal from your different directions. Let go and allow the full experience to wash over you, everything from breakfast cooked on a camp stove to crossing a stream on a rope bridge. You will gain a broader perspective on your job and both integrate and ingratiate yourself more fully with your Trail Life family.

Developing good character is ***why*** we work in Trail Life. Outdoor adventure and the patrol method are ***how*** we work. Keep this in mind as you consider that God's character is trinitarian, so it follows that the Image of a three-person God in us fully develops in the presence of ***relationships*** (*patrols and troops*) and that development is guided by the Patrol Method. The image of a God with so meaningful a relationship of persons would not lead us to a disengaged faith. Christianity is to some degree a "me" religion but in a much greater sense it is an "us" kind of faith, and character helps tie and tighten those bonds of Christian love.

Character is defined as the "Four Selves"; Self-Control, Self-Reliance, Self-Respect and Self-Worth. These are the four poles that support the canopy of character. Remove one and it sags… remove two and it collapses. Character also forms the Christian "Second Nature."

Self-Control: a Trailman *reacts* to grace by *acting* righteously. He *knows* that leadership starts within and he then *holds himself to the same standards* he expects from others. If you are not in control of your car, it is totally out of control?

Actually not…it's still subject to physical laws that care nothing about your desires or your safety. If you are not in control of your life, something else will be, and you won't like where it leads you.

Self-Reliance: a Trailman gives and accepts help as needed, avoiding the sin of being too proud. A Trailman is a valued team member who always contributes his fair share…or more. A Trailman must be a good steward of himself in order to best help others. When you are in danger or handling a crisis, you are the first person to realize it and the first person to mount a response. Obviously, you want that person to be a dedicated professional.

Self-Respect: a Trailman aspires to be more than he was yesterday and less than he'll be tomorrow. His self-respect resists moral diseases. "I would never do such a thing," he feels. Self-respect gives him moral authority to hold others to a high standard.

Self-Worth: Other youth organizations promote "self-esteem"; loving the person you are simply because you're unique. Trailmen joyfully remember that God loves and equips them uniquely to be useful. Self-worth reminds them they can also have self-control, self-reliance and self-respect. We must never blame our failures on how God made us or the sorts of opportunities He sends our way.

Character is especially important in a world that increasingly demands conformance. A Trailman seeks to conform with important expectations that tie all of us together. He would never seek to be in the image of anyone else but God. He would not conspire against his country or his faith. He would seek to be one with the Body of Christ and to remember in his memberships ranging from the Chess Club to the Church that, "There is no 'I' in 'TEAM'." And yet—and this is very important—he does not buy membership in any group that demands hatred of a race, language, culture or nationality. He does not feel compelled to wear certain clothes, drive certain cars, frequent certain venues, or engage in certain behaviors as the price of being accepted. He emulates his role models without slavishly imitating them. His voting record is not based on his age, sex, or address. In short, he is not a slave to circumstances or peer pressure. He takes credit for his successes, responsibility for his failures, and gives credit where credit is due, especially to his parents, his mentors, and God.

Getting to the true foundation of character is like getting to the foundation of a building. You have to dig deep through several layers of worthless material in search of something solid. Kent Marks, a contractor and Trail Life leader, tells the story of a builder who cast a huge concrete slab to foot a factory. The builder was upset when the slab cracked soon after drying. Upon investigation, he saw that his lot was a former city dump. At great cost, the spoiled concrete was removed, and steel piers were driven through the layers of buried soil and garbage to reach the underlying bedrock. Only then could a slab be laid that would support a factory. Our character is like that slab, and the four selves are the piers that rest on the foundation of Christ the solid rock. In His own words:

> *Therefore, everyone who hears these words of mine and puts them into practice is like a wise man who built his house on the rock. The rain came down, the streams rose, and the winds blew and beat against that house; yet it did not fall, because it had its foundation on the rock. But everyone who hears these words of mine and does not put them into practice is like a foolish man who built his house on sand. The rain came down, the streams rose, and the winds blew and beat against that house, and it fell with a great crash. -- Matthew 7:24-27*

First Nature comes naturally from our fallen humanity; panic, fear, hatred, pride, jealousy, greed and lust. These are the things we do in the absence of grace. First Nature is the empty lot where God wants to build a Christian Man. When He surveys it, it may be rough, overgrown, poorly drained and rocky. There may be a decaying house on it that needs to be replaced rather than repaired. That's okay...God understood that when He purchased it with Christ's blood. Yes, Jesus did dine with sinners, and he did speak with prostitutes, yet when He had finished with them, they were not the same people.

The boys your lead today also won't remain the same forever whether you intervene or not. Even a white fencepost that you think will stay white forever will someday need repainting or the old paint will turn gray and flake off. If simply left alone, conservative thought does not do any better than a talent of gold buried in the ground. It must be invested; it must grow if you are to be a good and faithful servant. Eternal, unchanging truths will continue to raise new harvests but only if the fields are well tended.

Second Nature is what you look to build. It comes from study, prayer and practice, yielding confidence, courage, forgiveness, humility, generosity and mercy. These are the things we only do when we make them ingrained habits through repetition.

Character Growth is akin to physical growth. The young Galahad must slay the dragon in his own castle before he can squire for a knight abroad and eventually become the mentor for squires of his own. We call our Trailmen "young men" for a perfectly good reason, yet remember children are not naïve adults in small bodies. They don't learn or reason like adults. They process the challenges and opportunities of life differently in a way that crosses cultural lines.

Toddlers from Kenya to Canada learn that obedience is rewarded, and disobedience is punished. Theirs is the morality of the Ten Comandments, a list of "thou shalts" and "thou shalt nots".

As the child gets older, they begin to understand and insist on fairness, their first major ideal. Theirs is the morality of the Golden Rule, to "Do unto others as you would have them do unto you." They begin to see that rewards and punishments are substitutes for younger boys that can't understand natural consequences.

Eventually they outgrow fairness and their grasp of abstract principles such as "patriotism" and "faith" ceases to be lists of rules. Older Trailmen have a deeper understanding of such phrases as "servant leadership" and "the price of freedom is not free." Theirs is the morality of the Good Samaritan, and it is the gold standard they achieve along the way to the Freedom Award. These boys are now living in an arch of character where each stone is busy holding up all the others and never has to worry about being held up itself.

Each of these three ages requires a different approach, and you will improve your ministry over time as you learn to recognize these age characteristics and develop a toolkit for dealing with them.

The Problems We Face

The majority of problems facing today's youth spring from the philosophical gulf between a people "created" and a people "emerged". This goes deeper than questioning the age of the earth or whether life changed over time; did our life come with a purpose or should it seek one? Are a created people moving away from a founding truth or are an emerged people running toward a golden age of humanistic thought? Should we define truth from the viewpoint of Jesus with one truth for all of us, or that of Pilate with one truth for each of us?

If life began randomly and evolved in a struggle to survive, we would be right to transcend biology at some point and seek our own purpose. It would make sense to equate morality with community acceptance. After all, why flee the dinosaurs when you can write novels?

Back in 1951, Robert Maynard Hutchins, Dean of Harvard Law School warned us of the dangers posed by spurning the wisdom of the created in favor of the philosophy of the emerged:

"Relativism, scientism, skepticism, and anti-intellectualism, the ***four horsemen of the philosophical apocalypse***, have produced that chaos in education which will end in the disintegration of the West."

So, who are these four horsemen?

- **Relativism:** The idea that notions of true and false, right and wrong, are purely subjective. The glorification of "tolerance" and the shift from pursuing truth and critical thinking to making students "college- and career-ready."
- **Scientism:** The idea that the only meaningful knowledge is gained through the scientific

method. That all life, beauty, feeling and purpose ultimately arose from the struggle of species to survive. That there is nothing ***unexplainable***, only the yet ***unexplained***.

- **Skepticism:** The idea that our beliefs are nothing more than our moods, humors and local prejudices. The viewpoint that none of our Western principles are superior to those of other cultures. The idea that what cannot be directly observed cannot be proven.
- **Anti-Intellectualism:** What Isaac Asimov called, "The false notion that democracy means that 'my ignorance is just as good as your knowledge.'" In today's schools, students are encouraged to have opinions on matters of which they have little to no knowledge. We are left with no hard and fast rules, but over 50 genders and the guarantee that we are the greatest experts on ourselves, able to self-identify ***who*** and ***what*** we are with total confidence based on how we feel and what we prefer.

The moral decline of the West started not in the 1960s but at the dawn of the twentieth century with the psychoanalytic musings of Sigmund Freud. The "flappers and sheiks" of the 1920s cited Freud in a pseudo-scientific campaign to liberate all manifestations of the sexual urge. That viewpoint was even codified by Chief Justice Oliver Wendell Holmes, Jr. who rejected absolutism (the distinction between natural and unnatural acts) in favor of moral relativism. Under his doctrine of "legal realism," legality was redefined to mean communal acceptability. In his dissenting opinion in the 1919 case "Abrams v. United States" he stated that the United States Constitution was "an experiment, as all life is an experiment," and added, "We should be eternally vigilant against attempts to check the expression of opinions that we loathe and believe to be fraught with death." We might be willing to risk that which is "fraught with death" for ourselves, but not for the children in our care! And is it right to wish for them the opinions that we "loathe" when they look to us for guidance? Do we have the right to call our efforts "raising" children if we put them on this path with nothing more substantive than "good wishes and happy trails"?

In the raging current of popular culture, people are too young to drive until they are 16, too young to be tried as an adult until they are 18, too young to drink until they are 21, but expected to choose if they want to go through life as a man or a woman by the time they are in third grade! Societal consensus may regard our morals as outdated, but they dare not call them arbitrary. At least we have a ***consistent*** consensus from setting anchor in the eternal truths.

Before the American Civil War people of color were counted as half a man each for the census. That begs the painful question—were people of color ever legally a half a man, or was societal consensus a half a truth? Even today a person magically turns from a "fetus" that can be legally aborted to a "baby" that can be criminally murdered simply by the act of being born. And the large number of progressive laws that make these and other ridiculous claims fall under "legal realism," as if they were the least bit in touch with law or reality. There yet remain courageous people who are ready to rebut this insanity for our children's sake, and as a chaplain you stand at the forefront.

A housefly makes a great show of brushing off its wings and face. Free of every trace of visible grime, the fly still spreads the germs it cannot see and does not believe in. Politically correct sinners are like that, caught in the mire of moral relativism, and they are steering our culture and setting our standards. Remember that young people are always judging their progress against standards. *Am I fast, slow, or average? Am I attractive or ugly?* When they turn to us for guidance, give worthy leadership by example. Ensure that your troop offers them the divine, historic standard of Christian manhood. Make sure they see modelled in its beliefs and practices the Christian husband, father, leader, teacher, friend and citizen.

Trailmen should aim to please God rather than their fellow men. In their quest to please God, they will automatically please the people who place their trust in Christ Jesus. Dr. Seuss famously said, "Be who you are and say what you feel, for those who truly matter don't mind, and those who mind don't truly matter." This becomes doctrinal when you remember that "being who you are" is discovering your true nature in Christ.

Social re-engineers want to replace a world built by created people with a new world built by emergent ones. Such a sea change in society requires plaining everything down to ground zero and starting over. We see that happening in many modern progressive theories about education and social harmony. They gleefully clear away churches and patrimony like slums to give them space to turn their blueprints into reality, but do we really want to live in their brash new city?

In 1789 France sent priests and their supporters to the guillotine as "enemies of the state". In 1926, Mexico waged the Cristero War against its Christian population. In both cases, the aim was ***to liberate mankind from "oppression by religion" and to "secure civil rights."*** Don't think it could never happen here. In the business world it already has. In the world of education, it happened long ago. Secular Humanists have erased Jesus from the public sphere by misappropriating Constitutional "separation of church and state". They did so not to avoid being "offended" by our beliefs, but secure in the knowledge that closed-doors religion is vulnerable and would hasten the attrition of churches that already has us speaking of the "post-Christian world".

Trail Life is Christianity bravely re-entering the public sphere. It will be met with resistance, but we don't care. As our Troops explore God's great outdoors, ever relevant life skills and historic Christian values in danger of being lost are easily, securely passed from parents to children.

If it's any consolation to you, this chapter was no more fun to write than it was to read. I wrote it and you read it for one reason only—we need to know what we are facing. But we also need to know what to do about it, and this is where your ministry makes a difference.

Our Response

Our response to the threats facing our young men is twofold.

First, we see the wonders of nature through the lens of God's word. The Bible is an important tool for discernment if we would take the advice from Job 12:7-10:

"But ask the animals, and they will teach you, or the birds in the sky, and they will tell you; or speak to the earth, and it will teach you, or let the fish in the sea inform you. Which of all these does not know that the hand of

the LORD has done this? In his hand is the life of every creature and the breath of all mankind."

In Romans 1:19-20, Paul tells us that through everything God made people can clearly see His invisible qualities, His eternal power and divine nature, which leaves them no excuse for not believing. The secular humanist, dead set against faith in any sort of God sees nature as nothing but a savage struggle for genetic survival.

In First Corinthians 1:18, Paul again tells us that the word of the cross is folly to those who are perishing, but to us who are being saved it is the power of God. The same is evidently true of the great truths God put into His creation. The ancient Greeks and Romans had the same lush forests, fragrant flowers, and shining rivers we enjoy. They looked upon them with awe and delight yet missed so much of their meaning, attributing to their gods the unpredictability of the natural forces around them. Many people today consider the levels of order and pattern in our biosphere the result of a few lucky hits from billions of failed experiments. No wonder Christ rebuked those who having eyes would not see and having ears would not hear!

Second, we leverage the relationship building skills of the Patrol Method to get the most out of our "minutes of ministry." The Patrol Method upbuilds the communal aspect of the image of God in each person.

Can you have a troop without the Patrol Method? Well yes, just like you can have a hospital without doctors, and with the same result! The Patrol Method is an intentional way to encourage Trailmen to lead themselves through self-control and to lead others through delegation, instruction and insight.

We all have a unique and personal relationship with God, and it follows that we also have a unique and personal relationship with the world He made. Young men share the excitement, drama and beauty of that relationship with their patrol family, which makes it even better.

The Patrol Method prepares the Trailman for the give-and-take nature of family life and the opportunities and discipline of a career. Central to youth leader training is the maxim that leadership is giving the gift of guidance. The Patrol Method starts with a Trailman's ability to discern and decide in his own life. The Patrol Method extends this ability to the patrol level, troop level, and the world. Just as you can't be a full Christian without interacting with the Church, you can't be a full Trailman without the Patrol Method. You may be good and idealistic, but Christianity and the Trail Life cry out for meaningful relationships built on trust and justified through Christ's injunction to love one another as He loved you.

The Role of the Troop Chaplain

Your job has seven major responsibilities. These are, in no particular order:

1. Be selected by, and remain accountable to, the Senior Ministry Leader's (SML) designee, the Troop Ministry Liaison (TML).
2. Ensure that the Troop keeps the spiritual development of youth in the forefront. Developing followers of Christ is at the heart of Trail Life. Faith is one of the six Program Emphases, and youth are encouraged to complete Faith Building Activities.

3. Create activities that emphasize spiritual awareness and development (such as planning devotions for campfires or Sunday morning worship services). Delegate and empower others to take the lead in those activities.
4. Mentor youth (chaplain aides, those pursuing religious awards, etc.), and approve those achievements once earned.
5. Encourage Trailmen to enter the Worthy Life program levels.
6. Keep Leaders and youth informed of opportunities to connect with other ministries within the host church, and in community outreach in general.
7. Seek connections and mentoring opportunities with dads who stay for meetings, but do not have leadership roles.

Prayer and Participation

As stated earlier, faith is not an opinion, a belief, or a philosophy. It should be active In the Troop. Patrols should start their meals with a blessing or giving thanks, and generally recognized religious days such as Sundays and Holidays should be properly acknowledged and observed. If they are not, be sure to point it out and see that things are put right. This is especially true of Trail Life Sunday, the second Sunday in September, which should be attended by all registered members in uniform where respectfully possible. Further, let your faith become action when the Troop is involved with service emphases such as, "Operation Christmas Child", "Respect Life", and "Attitude of Gratitude".

Some Good General Advice

When it is time to worship God on an outing, find a meeting place that is reasonably comfortable yet free of distractions. Tailor your message to the topic and location. Use simple, durable props that are easy to set up and break down. Avoid technology when possible.

Whatever you do, speak loudly, slowly and clearly. Make a habit of preaching to that short boy in the back row. No humor intended, visualize Lincoln giving the Gettysburg Address. Like him, you are being short, to the point, and speaking outdoors.

Involve other people so you will turn a sermon into a service. Give opportunities for young Trailmen to read scripture, handle props, or play another role. Music and Sacraments work well in a house made by God's own hands.

Note to Evangelicals

Once I attended Holy Communion served by a Baptist minister who forgot that grape juice comes into the world looking for ways to spoil. Very dutifully he filled all the small cups the night before and set them aside. At the most solemn moment in the ceremony, the preacher lifted the lid from the communion tray, said, "This is my blood which was shed for you," then glanced down and in a hushed voice asked me, "Does this look green to you?" I nodded. "Yes, I believe it is." Discretely he lowered the lid and said, "Let us pray." Then he made urgent gestures for me to refill the tray on the double. You may laugh now, but it wasn't so funny then. Don't be that minister.

Note to Catholic, Orthodox, and Anglican Celebrants

If you are new to this (as everyone is at least once), there is no need to ever bend or break eucharistic protocol on outings. Bring no more bread and wine than necessary and consume rather than conserve the consecrated host. There are communion kits made specially for outings that will help you concentrate on what's really important. Search for "Midsize Communion Kit for Travel" on www.almy.com or your preferred provider.

Chaplain Aide

One of the best ways you will mentor a young Trailman is to fully engage him as your Chaplain Aide. When he is working alongside you during a service, he is dramatically reminded that "A Trailman Honors God."

Chaplain Aide is a leadership position in the Troop. Someone may be tempted to accept the office simply to fulfil a leadership or service requirement, but that outcome would not benefit him, you, or the troop in the long run.

In addition to having an appropriate role at Troop worship services—such as handing out song lyrics and programs, reading scripture passages, or helping at services of Word and Table, it is appropriate to give the Chaplain Aide a part to play during the presentation of religious emblems or other religious commemorations. Encourage them to promote the religious emblem programs and ensure that opening prayers at leader meetings they attend are carried out.

If the Chaplain Aide has not earned a religious emblem or participated in a religious studies program such as "Worthy Life" or "Band of Brothers," encourage them to do so. Ask them to remember the Troop and Charter Organization in their personal prayers. Encourage them to consider faith activity trail badges.

Depending on how you handle it, the job can simply look good on a resume and fulfill a leadership or service requirement, or it can be a vital step along the path to Freedom Rangeman and ultimately Christian Man.

Confidentiality

Contrary to popular opinion, confidentiality is not intended to limit the sharing of information, it is intended to promote it. It has been said that we all have a different face behind the mask we wear, and it is this face you must see if you are going to help the Trailman he truly is rather than the Trailman he appears to be. The assurance of confidentiality gives you a chance to see what you must see in order to know how to say, pray, and do the right thing.

Unless you are told something that has an immediate effect on his health and safety, or the health and safety of others, whatever is shared with you should stay with you.

If you are dealing with medical information protected under the 1996 Health Insurance Portability & Accountability Act (HIPAA), federal law requires you to strictly follow patient privacy guidelines. This will affect what you can share about the patient, and what permissions you need in order to update the Troop or visit patients in a hospital.

Let's be clear on this:

- If your client tells you he has set a booby trap, plans to harm himself, or to harm someone else in any way, there are reporting requirements you must meet that override your concerns about confidentiality.
- If you have been told that your client has been subjected to abuse—mental, physical, sexual, emotional or neglect—or you have reason to suspect that this is the case, you ***must*** follow the reporting requirements of your state while also adhering to the procedures set out by Trail Life Health and Safety Guide.
- Anything that takes place in a hospital or clinic setting, including a diagnosis or prognosis or treatment regimen can only be revealed with the patient's or guardian's approval.

Credentialing Requirements

If you want to perform hospital or clinic visits, it is necessary for you to establish credibility as a chaplain. The way different healthcare venues go about this varies not only from state to state but facility to facility.

Chaplains should check with the Hospital administrators before making regular hospital visits. Most hospitals have a formal training class for chaplains. After completing the specific training, usually the hospital will issue you a badge, so the hospital staff knows that you are familiar with the HIPAA rules. Basically, the rule is do not disclose a patient's personal information with anyone.

Fully three quarters of patients hold some sort of belief in the effect of prayer on illness, so there is significant pressure on the healthcare community to treat chaplains as a member of the medical care team. Access to the patient, the diagnosis, the prognosis and the treatment options will be shared to a greater or lesser degree depending upon the jurisdiction. That pressure does not always have direct effect, yet all hospitals and clinics are aware of the important role of patient morale to healing. Gaining the trust of hospital administration is a small price to pay in order to bring the comfort of prayer and a sympathetic ear into the patient's room.

Counseling

One of your main jobs is counseling, something that is important for two reasons. Yes, you need to prevent logistical bumps in the patrol and troop caused by disciplinary problems, but more importantly you want to promote growth of faith and character. If you want a professional, well-disciplined outing, go hiking with the Sierra Club. If you want absence of strife, build a church on the dark side of the moon, far away from human beings and their neediness. These are youths you are evangelizing, works in progress. They are not here to showcase their perfection but rather to grow toward it. Thanks to you, that growth will be steady and rightly guided.

Disciplinary Cases

By the time a disciplinary case reaches you, it will have already been filtered through the Trailman's Patrol Leader, Second Officer, First Officer and probably Troopmaster. Your primary task is to deal with the bad feelings that arise from passing the buck so many times and from all the approaches that failed. It is good at a time like this to remember how the Lord's Prayer starts by saluting and praising God and acknowledging His will for your life before you start asking for things. Open your session with a non-judgmental prayer that begins with thanking God and asking His blessings on all involved. Move from there to asking God's guidance in bringing a solution to the situation that will help everyone to go and grow. See if you can find the underlying cause in an unresolved resentment, fear or uncertainty. You should never attempt to diagnose a possible mental health problem, and you need to remember that you are acting in your role as a Trail Life leader and under the same constraints of authority that go with our system of constructive discipline.

Difficult Questions and Doubts

Most Trailmen will be someone looking for answers either to a simple problem or one of life's great questions. As you gain experience, you'll come to realize that these are often the same thing presented in different ways. See the chapter on Difficult Questions.

Trailmen are also quite afraid of the questions most Christians feel at some point about the validity of their faith. Moments of doubt are a normal part of the human condition in this fallen world, and it is helpful to remind them of Christ's promise, "Seek and ye shall find." These moments of doubt make them human, not evil.

Spiritual Comfort

A chaplain may also be asked to bring comfort to those suffering from nightmares, fear of the dark, fear of the unknown, and on first long outings a bout of homesickness. Be quick to point out that fear is a gift from God that steers us away from danger, but like all gifts He gives us, we must use it rather than be used by it. Cowardice is not the absence of fear, it is how we relate to it and what we do about it. No, there is not a monster under the cot. Once that becomes clear, the fear will go away on its own. As for homesickness, remember that model airplane you built as a boy...the parts had to be held together long enough for the glue to harden. Outdoor adventure is the glue that keeps Trailmen in the wildwood, and many leaders praise the advice, "Can you stay for one more day? If you still want to go home tomorrow evening, we'll call your folks." That call almost never happens, and it only happens with the assent of the Troopmaster—it's not your judgment call.

Intervention

Trail Life has declared bullying and hazing of all sorts to be unacceptable and has established policy and practice to prevent it when possible, and to deal with it when it occurs. Remember the words often attributed to Edward Burk that "The only thing necessary for evil to triumph is for good men to remain silent". By the time a Trailman reaches the Hawk age group, he understands that there are three basic types of people; sheep, wolves and sheepdogs. When wolves desire to prey upon sheep, they are confronted by the sheepdog. When even one person takes up for a victim of bullying, the bad behavior usually stops at once. Chaplains should be able to recognize and quickly intervene in cases of suspected bullying.

Abuse

Your role in handling abuse is circumscribed yet vital. If a Trailman comes to you to report abuse, whether sexual, physical, emotional or neglect, it is your duty to follow your state's laws on reporting and to take actions prescribed in the Trail Life Health and Safety Guide. You are also required to report your good faith suspicions of abuse. You should not try to investigate it yourself.

Difficult Questions

When you have been a Chaplain long enough, you'll encounter the difficult questions that young people ask. Some of them will sound flippant, yet behind nearly every one of them is the hope you will have the magic key that opens the lock. Probably you as an adult will hear them from a troubled boy who is dealing with a crisis of faith.

There is not always one perfect answer to every question, but here are a few of the ones I've heard over the years and how I dealt with them.

Can God make a rock too big for Him to move?

This one has frightened generations of young people! After all, the answer "yes" or "no" alike opens a limit on God's all-powerful nature, yet its power hinges on our limited human understanding of infinity. Point out that God could create an infinitely large rock that was simultaneously out of places to go yet was anywhere He wanted it to be. That answer points out how ridiculous the question is.

If God is all powerful and good, why is there evil in the world?

This is the one you hate to hear, because it hints both at cracks in God's abilities and in His willingness to use them for good. And while there is no simple logical answer to the question of evil, you can at least reassure your Trailmen that God is in control.

The scriptures tell us that all of nature has suffered from the fall of man and waits in groaning for the New Creation. It has, like us, been redeemed by Christ's death and resurrection, but not yet remade. That means this world, like us, is a work in progress. Progress is messy.

That's similar to the way mother always keeps a clean kitchen unless food is being prepared. Then it can be very dirty, with flour on the countertops, dishes piled in the sink, and greasy pans on the stove. Will it be hard to clean? You bet! So why get it dirty in the first place if you only have to clean it again? To cook steak and cake and fresh corn muffins! Why have a kitchen in the first place if it must not be dirty for a single instant? God could have avoided sending His Son to the cross by not making man in His image. The fact that He did it knowing what it would cost Him, says a lot about more about the character of God's power and goodness than hurricanes, epidemics and earthquakes.

I prayed for God to let Grandma live, but she died!

God answers our prayers the way he answers our questions—yes, no or maybe.

Imagine that you are standing in a crowd of a thousand people. And all of those people are going to Camp Heaven with you. Great! Problem is, you have one bus that holds fifty passengers at a time. It will have to make the long trip to Heaven and back twenty times to get everyone there! Your grandmother might be on the first trip, your sister might ride with you, and you may have to let your children take the next bus. People will end up being separated for many years, but the wait is worth it. Waiting to see your loved ones again is one of the hardest things you'll ever do, but at least it's temporary if Christ is your travel agent.

In general, there are times when God thinks it better to answer your prayer the way you would have prayed it if you had possessed His wisdom and unselfishness. Think about the man who was running late. “Please God, don’t let me miss the train!” He missed the train anyhow and with it a chance for a good job, and that made him quite upset at God. Later, when he heard that the train crashed and many passengers had died, he was sorry for being angry. Rarely will it be so clear cut. The vast majority of “unanswered” prayers help us in ways we will never begin to understand. Just be certain that God doesn’t enjoy telling the people He loves, “No.” He only does it for a good reason.

But it’s not fair!

The unfairness of this fallen world hurts us all. It won’t always be like that. Just remember that God was hurt worst of all, to have to send his blameless Son into the world to live the life you couldn’t live and die the death you would have died. There are a lot of times in life when you just have to cry. That’s okay. Remember always that God has His hand on your shoulder, crying along with you.

Am I good enough to go to Heaven?

Good news, son...nobody is! We enter Heaven because of Christ's goodness. That does not mean you shouldn't try to be the very best person you can be.

Have I committed the unforgivable sin?

Blasphemy against the Holy Spirit is something we don't fully understand, but we know you wouldn't be frightened by it if you had actually done it or you were the type who would.

Did the Jews kill Jesus?

That's like asking if the Americans shot Abraham Lincoln. Being Jewish does not mean agreeing with High Priest Caiphas any more than being American means agreeing with John WIlkes Booth. Do many Jews think Jesus wasn't the Son of God? Yes, but that's also how many Hindus think, and they didn't kill Him either. The real question should be, "Is it ever right to kill someone for believing differently?" and most of today's Jews and Christians would rightly answer, "No!"

"Science v. Faith"

Young people are often very interested in the relationship of faith and science, something dealt with at length in John Paul II's helpful encyclical, "Fides et Ratio" (Faith and Reason) that concludes faith and reason are the wings that work together to allow our souls to fly.

There are different viewpoints even within faith traditions over old earth versus young earth, and whether or not living things change over time. Each of these viewpoints may bring people feelings of comfort or awe for a variety of reasons but being curious about natural history is not the same as trying to remove God from His throne. Where all Christians agree is that without God's wisdom, power and will, you would not be here.

Specific doctrinal questions

You may have Trailmen from differing faith traditions in your Troop. Unless you are co-religionists, please refer denomination-specific questions to his parents or clergy. If parents feel you are abusing your position of authority and influence, they will either complain about you or pull their son from the troop.

Why go to church?

Christianity has congregations the way Trail Life Troops have patrols. They are places where the Triune aspect of the Image of God in you is strengthened through relationships. They are places where you learn and practice leadership. They are an avenue of grace where the Holy Spirit shows up as two or three gather together in Christ's name. They are places of learning, accountability, fellowship, encouragement and mutual aid. They are places of blessings and sacraments. They are worthy models of other relationships we have such as marriages, careers, citizenships, and friendships.

What are miracles?

A miracle would seem to be something that suspends or violates the laws of nature. Yet nature's "laws" are not like the Ten Commandments or even your national or local laws. They are descriptions of closed systems, much like a wall clock. Within a clock, "laws" dictate that one complete revolution of the minute hand moves the hour hand a twelfth of the way around the dial. Then one day it is time for daylight savings to start, and a finger from outside the system unexpectedly intervenes to turn the minute hand a complete revolution backwards! There is nothing in the laws of clockwork to explain such a thing—it shouldn't even be possible. To the clock, this act is a miracle because the hand is not part of its clock universe. The "otherness" of God to our universe causes our systems to work in new and unexpected ways. It's not magic, it's intervention.

It's all my fault!

Children sometimes blame themselves when the adults in their lives don't get along. This can be especially devastating when parents invoke the natural frustrations of caregivers into the argument. Jim heard his parents having a fight about getting a divorce, and in the heat of battle, his mother shouted, "You can always get away to go fishing, but you ***NEVER*** come to Jimmy's soccer games!" Without going into detail, the discussion of Jim heads downhill, alleging how Mom is always spoiling him and interfering with discipline. Jim feels this must be all his fault.

He needs to know that parents say things when they are angry that they wouldn't say—and more importantly, ***wouldn't feel***—otherwise. It is not up to children to make their parents' marriage work. Parents are adults, and if they can't work through things, it's certainly not the fault of a 12-year-old acting like a boy. "They both really love you," you can also remind him. "Jim, no matter what happens, they will always be your Mom and Dad. Let's pray about it, ok?"

Anything else you can't answer

"I don't know," followed by, "Let's find out." Then do it.

Faith Building Options

Trail Life USA is a character, leadership, and adventure organization for boys and young men. An unapologetically Christian organization, its leaders sign and adhere to a Trinitarian Christian Statement of Faith and Values as part of their membership application.

Youth members, though not required to accept Christianity, are expected to adhere to Christian standards of behavior.

Spiritual emphases are woven throughout every level of the program while we aspire to include robust adventure. The familiar analogy is like the carrot in carrot cake. You may not find huge chunks of Bible teachings in the everyday process of the Trail Life USA program, but the elements are there in every bite!

Our concept is that boys will be drawn to the adventure while adults will appreciate the Christian influence and traditional biblical and family values. Trail Life USA is Unapologetically Christ-centered.

The K-12 programs of Trail Life USA encourage outdoor experiences that build a young man's skills and allow him to grow on a personal level and as a role model and leader of his peers. Living the Trail Life is a journey established on timeless values derived from the Bible.

Following are some of the foundational statements and tenets that establish our spiritual emphasis:

Statement of Faith

We believe there is One Triune God – God the Father; Jesus Christ, His one and only Son; and the Holy Spirit– Creator of the universe and eternally existent. We believe the Holy Scriptures (Old and New Testaments) to be the inspired and authoritative Word of God. We believe each person is created in His image for the purpose of communing with and worshiping God. We believe in the ministry of the Holy Spirit, who enables us to live godly lives. We believe each of us is called to love the Lord our God with all our heart, mind, soul, and strength, and to love our neighbors as ourselves. We believe God calls us to lives of purity, service, stewardship and integrity.

Statement of Values

Purity: God calls us to lives of holiness, being pure of heart, mind, word and deed. We are to reserve sexual activity for the sanctity of marriage, a lifelong commitment before God between a man and a woman.

Service: God calls us to become responsible members of our community and the world through selfless acts that contribute to the welfare of others.

Stewardship: God calls us to use our God-given time, talents, and money wisely.

Integrity: God calls us to live moral lives that demonstrate an inward motivation to do what is biblically right regardless of the cost.

Vision

Our vision is to be the premier national character development organization for young men which produces Godly and responsible husbands, fathers, and citizens.

Mission

Our mission is simple and clear: to guide generations of courageous young men to honor God, lead with integrity, serve others, and experience outdoor adventure.

Oath

On my honor, I will do my best; to serve God and my country; to respect authority; to be a good steward of creation; and to treat others as I want to be treated.

Motto

"Walk Worthy" From Colossians 1:9-10

Core Value #1 – Christ Centered

Trail Life USA (TLUSA) is a Christian Outdoor adventure program that emphasizes and teaches biblical moral values and requires all adult members to agree with, sign, and abide by the Trail Life USA Trinitarian Statement of Faith and the Statement of Values. The program is unapologetically Christian. However, the program is designed and intended to be presented without being churchy or religious, focusing on outdoor adventure, character, and leadership development. The analogy for this principle has been referred to as carrot cake. The carrots in the cake are not in big and obvious chunks, but are still present throughout the entire cake, as are the assumptions of a Christian worldview throughout the entire program. At the same time, the TLUSA program is not intended to replace or compete with other youth groups, Bible studies, or church programs, but rather to complement them and give youth an opportunity to exemplify and demonstrate Christian values in their relationships with others. (For a complete list of Core Values, see https://www.traillifeusa.com/core-values/

Faith building opportunities are present at every level of the program and inherent in our purposes. We expect God to make Himself known, and endeavor to create every opportunity possible for boys to acknowledge and grow in their knowledge of Him. The following spiritual growth options are integrated into the Trail Life program ***in addition*** to the adventure, character, and leadership development requirements and skills that are inherent in the path from Fox to Freedom.

The Faith Section of the "6 F's" Lesson Plans (WT)

Each lesson of the Woodlands Trail contains a faith building nugget for the Trail Guide leader to discuss with the Trailmen.

Values Branch Award (WT)

Values (one of the seven Woodlands Trail Branches) is for instilling a Bible-based system of values regarding a number of pertinent topics. A central focus of this branch is the teachings of the Christian faith.

Worthy Life Award (WT)

The Worthy Life Award can be earned at each level of the Woodlands Trail Program (Fox, Hawk, and Mountain Lion). It involves completion of certain faith-centered activities, projects, or accomplishments. The requirements earned are age group specific. For Fox, "Who is God?", "God Loves Me!". For Hawk, "My Faith and Belief", "My Neighbor," and "My Family." For Mountain Lion, "My Family," "My Community," and "Biblical Manhood." The Worthy Life Award is worn on the left pocket flap of the Trail Life uniform.

Timberline Award (WT)

This is the highest award a Trailman can achieve in the Woodlands Trail program. It was developed to celebrate a boy's bridging into the new world of the Navigator's program. There are four Manhood Principles and requirements: (a) to live boldly and avoid being passive, (b) to live responsibly, (c) to lead courageously, and (d) to live for the greater rewards of God.

Religious Recognitions (WT)

These religious recognitions may be worn on the uniform on the left pocket:

<table>
<tr><th>Theme:
Knowledge
Values
Branch
(Faith)</th><th>Worthy Life</th><th colspan="2">Religious Recognitions
(detailed below)</th></tr>
<tr><td rowspan="2">Fox (K-1)
Noah's Ark</td><td rowspan="2">Who is God?
God Loves Me!</td><td>Catholic</td><td>Other</td></tr>
<tr><td>NCCTL – Family of God (Our Father)</td><td rowspan="2">MCCES – Loving Servant
EOCS – St. George</td></tr>
<tr><td>Hawk (2-3)
Bible</td><td>My Faith & Belief,
My Neighbor
and
My Family</td><td>NCCTL – Family of God (His Mercy Endures Forever)</td></tr>
<tr><td>Mountain Lion (4-5)
Cross</td><td>My Family,
My Community,
and
Biblical Manhood</td><td colspan="2">EOCS – Chi-Rho
MCCS – Joyful Servant
NCCTL – Family of God (I Shall Not Fear)</td></tr>
<tr><td colspan="4">Timberline Award: Four Manhood Principles – (a) to live boldly and avoid being passive, (b) to live responsibly, (c) to lead courageously, and (d) to live for the greater rewards of God.</td></tr>
</table>

Religious Recognitions (NAV)

Ready Trailmen must complete one of the following Faith-building Activity options:

- **Any Values (red) Trail Badge:** Values Trail Badges can be completed by either Christian or non-Christian boys. The Bible Basics Badge is focused on learning through participation and study and may be done in the family, unit, or church setting at the discretion of the boy's family. Additional Values Trail Badges are planned.
- **Trail Life USA Worthy Life Award:** Working with an adult leader who will disciple him, the candidate will participate in an individualized or group discipleship program with a minimum duration of three months. All meetings with the adult leader should adhere to the Trail Life Child Safety and Youth Protection guidelines. This program allows the youth, his family and mentor to determine the materials used. It may accommodate study programs the youth may already be involved with outside Trail Life.

- **Manhood Journey:** This dynamic program is a two-year interdenominational Bible-based approach to building young men through the discipleship and mentorship of their own father and/or other adult males in the program. The purpose of the Manhood Journey is to provide a Christian discipleship program for our Troops aimed at building young men spiritually through Bible study and faith mentorship.

Those Religious Recognitions shown below may be worn on the uniform on the left pocket:

<table>
<tr><th>Ranks Theme: Understanding</th><th>Spiritual Study Options</th><th>Religious Recognitions (detailed below)</th><th colspan="2">Discipleship Program</th></tr>
<tr><td>Recruit Trailman</td><td rowspan="3">Any Values Frontier Elective Trail Badge</td><td rowspan="3">EOCS – Alpha Omega
MCCS – Good Servant
NCCTL – Brothers in Christ</td><td rowspan="3">Worthy Life</td><td rowspan="3">Manhood Journey</td></tr>
<tr><td>Able Trailman</td></tr>
<tr><td>Ready Trailman</td></tr>
<tr><td></td><td colspan="4">Values Frontier Elective Trail Badges
Developed as optional faith-focused Trail Badges for Navigators and Adventurers</td></tr>
</table>

Religious Recognitions (ADV)

Freedom Rangemen must complete one of the following Faith-building Activity options:

- **Trail Life Worthy Life Award:** Working with an adult leader who will disciple him, the candidate will participate in an individualized or group discipleship program with a maximum duration of three months. All meetings with the adult leader must adhere to Trail Life's Child Safety and Youth Protection guidelines. This program allows the youth, his family and mentor to determine the materials used. It may accommodate study programs the youth may already be involved with outside Trail Life. The Worthy Life Award is worn on the left pocket flap of the uniform.

- **Trail Life Band of Brothers:** The Band of Brothers provides a Christian discipleship focused program aimed at building young men spiritually through Bible study and faith mentorship. As an intermediate experience in discipleship, the Band of Brothers program has young men disciple other young men in Christian growth and learning under the guidance of adult mentors. While the programming is intended for discipleship among young men, adult mentors play a role of guiding each Band of Brothers group.
- **Trail Life Vanguard Program:** An intense service and discipleship opportunity for the brightest and most deeply devoted Christian young men in Trail Life. Through Vanguard we are creating a

culture and a cadre of young men who are on fire for Jesus Christ, who are excellent leaders, and who are passionate about serving God through Trail Life. The program is in pilot review mode.

These religious recognitions may be worn on the uniform on the left pocket:

<table>
<tr><th>Awards Theme: Wisdom</th><th>Religious Recognitions (detailed below)</th><th colspan="3">Discipleship Program</th></tr>
<tr><td>Journey Trailman</td><td>EOCS – Alpha Omega</td><td rowspan="3">Worthy Life</td><td rowspan="3">Band of Brothers</td><td></td></tr>
<tr><td>Horizon Trailman</td><td>MCCS – Giving Servant</td><td rowspan="2">Vanguard Program (10-12)</td></tr>
<tr><td>Freedom Rangeman</td><td>NCCTL – Christ the King
NCCTL – Sword of St. Michael</td></tr>
<tr><td colspan="5">Adventurers Freedom Experiences: Christian Education</td></tr>
</table>

Freedom Experiences

At the high school level in the Adventurers Program, a Trailman is encouraged to participate in citizenship experiences in the community. One of the Freedom Experience fields of study is Christian Education.

Catholic Faith Options

The National Catholic Committee of Trail Life USA (NCCTL) is working to provide a series of strong Catholic religious emblems. Catholic options may be selected for completing the Worthy Life Award for Navigators as well as the Worthy Life Award and Band of Brothers options for Adventurers as these programs use materials approved by Charter Organizations, parents and Troop leaders.

Religious Recognition Emblems

These awards are focused on helping a youth understand the basics of his denominational faith tradition (i.e. major doctrinal positions, church history, the importance of participation).

- **NCCTL – National Catholic Committee of Trail Life USA** – www.CatholicTrail.org – Emblems are in development at time of printing.
- **EOCS – Eastern Orthodox Committee on Scouting** – www.eocs.org – Materials and awards for St. George, Chi-Rho and Alpha and Omega.
- **MCCS – Members of Churches of Christ for Scouting** – www.goodservant.org or call 325-370-1679 – Materials and awards for *Loving Servant, Joyful Servant, Good Servant*, and *Giving Servant*.
- **P.R.A.Y – Programs of Religious Activities With Youth** – www.praypub.org or call 800-933-7729 – Materials and awards for *Jesus and Me, God and Me, God and Family, God and Church, and God and Life*.

Woodland Trails Values Branch Awards

The Purpose and Skills Progression for each step is printed here for your reference. Helps, Activity Ideas, Game Ideas and Scriptures accompany this information on the Values Branch program sheets available online at Trail Life Connect.

Notes to Trail Guides:

- The goal is not for the boys to become experts at these topics, but rather for them to gain an increased knowledge and awareness of each step.
- Make it relative to your patrol.
- Remember, these lessons should build from Fox to Hawk and from Hawk to Mountain Lion.
- See the Woodlands Trail Leaders Guide for more information on Steps.

Step One – Godly Values

Purpose

The 'Godly Values' step provides a basic knowledge of what Values are and the benefit of having and living by values based upon Godly principles. Upon completion of this step, Trailmen should understand where our values come from and why they are important.

1. What are values?
2. Name some values.
3. How do values affect our lives?
4. Name some places we get our values.
5. What is the benefit of having Godly values?

Skills Progression

Fox

1. Know what a value is and where it comes from.
2. Focus on values: Attentiveness and Obedience.
3. Doing a job well at home.

Hawk

1. Know where our values come from.

2. Focus on the values: Honor and Diligence.
3. Doing a job well at home and school.

Mountain Lion

1. Know where our values come from.
2. Focus on the values: Diligence and Discernment.
3. Doing a job well.

Step Two – Our Faith and Values

Purpose

The 'Our Faith' step provides a basic knowledge and understanding of what faith is and its practical application. Upon completion of this step, Trailmen should understand how we can use our faith to serve and help others around us as well as the biblical foundation of lasting faith and the importance of placing one's faith in God who is trustworthy.

1. What is faith?
2. Why is it important to place our faith or trust in Jesus?
3. How does our faith affect our values?
4. Name some values we get from our faith.

5. Why is faith important to our system of values?
6. Find an instance in the Bible where a value is defined. Discuss it.

Skills Progression

Fox

1. Learn about believing in something that we do not see.
2. Importance of respect in our home.

Hawk

1. Importance of putting our faith in God always, even when things don't go our way.
2. Importance of showing respect in home, school, and the places we go.

Mountain Lion

1. How do we grow in our faith and share our faith with others?
2. Importance of showing respect to others. Learn the Golden Rule and how to apply it.

Step Three – Godly Citizenship

Purpose

The 'Godly Citizenship' step provides a basic introduction to the concept of a Christian Worldview and how the Trailman can influence their world in a positive, Godly direction. Upon completion of this step, a Trailman should understand how his actions influence his community and his witness.

1. What does it mean to be a Godly citizen?
2. Define what it means to have a Christian Worldview.
3. What are some actions of a Godly citizen?
4. Discuss how we can be involved in our government, school, and community as part of being a godly citizen.
5. Good opportunity for Hit the Trail to participate in a government, school or community activity as a Godly influence.

Skills Progression

Fox

1. Godly citizenship begins at home.
2. Learning how to honor father and mother and responding to them with immediate obedience.

Hawk

1. How can we be a Godly citizen at home, school, and community?
2. Learning to do the things in the Trailman Oath in preparation for future leadership.

Mountain Lion

1. Emphasis here on community service and how we can be involved in the community and local government.
2. Learning to be a leader and helping others.

Elective Nine – Righteousness

Purpose

The purpose of 'Righteousness' is to introduce the Trailman to the concept of Right Living despite one's situation or surroundings. Upon completion of this objective, Trailmen should understand the importance and practical application of this Character trait.

1. What is Righteousness?
2. How can we know what is the right way to live or act in different circumstances?
3. How does the Bible provide a consistent standard for living despite one's situation or surroundings?
4. What are some activities that can build our understanding of right living?
5. How did the sacrifice of Jesus make us right in the presence of a Holy God?
6. What are some ways we can encourage others to be and live righteously?

Skills Progression

Fox

1. Learn the meaning of righteousness.
2. Learn where righteousness comes from.

Hawk

1. Learn how righteousness looks in life.
2. Learn about biblical people who demonstrated righteousness.

Mountain Lion

1. Learn how to recognize righteousness in others.
2. Learn how to live more righteously.

Elective Twelve – Repentance

Purpose

The purpose of 'Repentance' is to introduce the Trailman to the concept of being sorry and changing one's actions and attitude. Upon completion of this objective, Trailmen should understand the importance and practical application of this Character trait.

1. What is Repentance?
2. Was there a time in your life that you realized you were going the wrong way, stopped, and turned around?
3. What are some examples of times when repentance can be important?

4. What does it take to repent?
5. What are examples from history of men that have repented, changing their actions and attitude?

Skills Progression

Fox

1. What is the meaning of Repentance?
2. Why do we repent?

Hawk

1. How do we pray for repentance?
2. How the people in the Bible repented.

Mountain Lion

1. What other things come with repentance?
2. What is your role in the repentance of others?

Elective Thirteen – Respect Life

Purpose

The purpose of 'Respect Life' is to teach the Trailmen that life is precious and wonderfully made.

1. What does it mean to be created in the Image of God?
2. What is redemption and why do we need it?
3. What is compassion and why do we need it?
4. When does human life start?

Skills Progression

Fox

1. God is the original and perfect image.
2. God formed us and made us.
3. Jesus mirrors a perfect image as a human.
4. Life is precious and wonderful.

Hawk

1. We are reflections of God's Image.
2. Our image has been distorted.
3. Jesus paid our debt.
4. Everyone deserves compassion.

Mountain Lion

1. God has fearfully and wonderfully made us.
2. Sin is on all of us.
3. Sin tempts us any time we are not focused on God.
4. Compassion allows us to be better image bearers.

Woodlands Trails Heritage Branch – Christian Heritage

The Purpose and Skills Progression for Step 1 – Christian Heritage - is printed here for your reference. Helps, Activity Ideas, Game Ideas and Scriptures accompany this information on the Heritage Branch program sheet available online at Trail Life Connect.

Notes to Trail Guides:

- The goal is not for the boys to become experts at these topics, but rather for them to gain an increased knowledge and awareness of each step.
- Make it relative to your patrol.
- Remember, these lessons should build from Fox to Hawk and from Hawk to Mountain Lion.
- See the Woodlands Trail Leaders Guide for more information on Steps.

Step One – Christian Heritage

Purpose

The 'Christian Heritage' step provides a basic knowledge of the history of Christianity as documented in the Bible. Upon completion of this step, Trailmen should be exposed to how the doctrines and tradition explained in the Bible apply to our Christian walk.

1. Who is Jesus?
2. In your own words, what is the Christmas story?
3. Who is a character in the Bible and how did God use him or her?
4. Who is a church hero (not in the Bible) and why is he or she significant?
5. Who was an example of a Christian martyr and why did he or she die?
6. What is the importance of prayer?
7. How should we pray?

Skills Progression

Fox

1. Understand who Jesus is and why he came to earth.
2. Be able to identify several biblical and historical figures.
3. Appreciate the importance of prayer.

Hawk

1. Understand who Jesus is and why he came to earth.
2. Be able to identify several Biblical and historical figures.
3. Appreciate the importance of prayer.
4. Memorize the Lord's Prayer.

Mountain Lion

1. Be able to clearly tell another person who Jesus is.
2. Pray regularly for troop, leaders, and fellow Trailmen.

Worthy Life Award

Trail Life USA is a Christ-centered outdoor adventure, leadership, and character development ministry. Within the operations of the local Troop, the primary statement/profession of Christian beliefs, faith, and/or doctrine is that belonging to the Charter Organization. As with any of its ministries, the Charter Organization should take steps to ensure the Troop appropriately reflects these beliefs. Furthermore, all Trail Life USA Charter Organizations and Registered Adult Members must concurrently adhere to the Christian principles stated in the Trail Life USA's Statements of Faith and Values, and all activities must be completed in conformity with Youth Protection Guidelines.

Any Bible Study Program should agree with your Charter Organization's Faith Tradition. This may include Christian Religious Recognition Programs.

It is highly recommended to select and use materials that encourage at least one session to be completed at home, led by a parent or guardian.

Woodlands Trail Fox

To achieve the Woodlands Trail Fox Worthy Life Award, you must complete the requirements in all four areas below with your parent(s) as well as your Trail Guides and/or Troop Chaplain as an active Trail Life USA Fox:

1. A Devotional Activity
2. A Discipleship Activity
3. Disciplines Activities
4. Demonstration Activities

The Devotional and Discipleship Activities are where Trailmen will choose, learn, and explore biblical principles. The Disciplines Activities are where the Trailmen apply their new knowledge to their lives. The Demonstration Activity is where the Trailman reports on his experiences to his peers and leaders. These activities may overlap with each other and should be integrated together when possible. Ensure that all completion dates are correctly documented in the Woodlands Trail Handbook and on www.TrailLifeConnect.com.

1. Devotional Activity

Participate in one (1) of the following activities with your parent(s) as well as your Trail Guides and/or Troop Chaplain:

- An age-appropriate Bible study program consisting of at least six (6) 20-minute sessions. Topics should focus on basic knowledge and skills of the Christian life, such as an introduction to the Bible, its main characters, God's creation, its major themes (Faith, Love, Prayer, Sacrifice, etc.), as well as Trail Life core themes of honor, respect, stewardship, and treatment of others.
- Four (4) additional Values Branch Elective Steps.

2. Discipleship Activity

Participate in one (1) of the following activities and discuss it with your parent(s) as well as your Trail Guides and/or Troop Chaplain:

- Read a story or watch a video about the life of a Bible character.
- Participate in a service project.
- Build a craft or project related to your Devotional Activity.

3. Disciplines Activities

Complete all three (3) of the following activities with your parent(s) as well as your Trail Guides and/or Troop Chaplain:

- Memorize and recite at least three (3) Scripture verses, prayers, hymns, creeds, and/or catechisms discussed during the Devotional Activity.
- Lead a prayer at mealtime with your family and during a Trail Life event.
- Attend a special church service or mass: Christmas, Good Friday, Easter, etc.

4. Demonstration Activities

Complete both of the following activities with your Trail Guides and/or Troop Chaplain:

- Recite for your patrol and/or Trail Guide the three memory passages from the Disciplines Activities
- Hold a final conference explaining what you have experienced and learned through the Worthy Life Award.

Woodlands Trail Hawk

To achieve the Woodlands Trail Hawk Worthy Life Award, you must complete the requirements in all four areas below with your parent(s) as well as your Trail Guides and/or Troop Chaplain as an active Trail Life USA Hawk:

1. A Devotional Activity
2. A Discipleship Activity
3. Disciplines Activities
4. Demonstration Activities

The Devotional and Discipleship Activities are where Trailmen will choose, learn, and explore biblical principles. The Disciplines Activities are where the Trailmen apply their new knowledge to their lives. The Demonstration Activity is where the Trailman reports on his experiences to his peers and leaders. These activities may overlap with each other and should be integrated together when possible. Ensure that all completion dates are correctly documented in the Woodlands Trail Handbook and on www.TrailLifeConnect.com.

1. Devotional Activity

Participate in one (1) of the following activities with your parent(s) as well as your Trail Guides and/or Troop Chaplain:

- An age appropriate Bible study program consisting of at least eight (8) 30-minute sessions. Topics should focus on basic knowledge and skills of the Christian life, such as neighborly love, mercy, grace, salvation, family, Bible organization, biblical character studies, as well as the principles set forth in the Trail Life motto and mission.
- Four (4) additional Values Branch Elective Steps.

2. Discipleship Activities

Participate in two (2) of the following activities and discuss them with your parent(s) as well as your Trail Guides and/or Troop Chaplain:

- Read a story or watch a video about the life of a church leader or missionary.
- Participate in a service project.
- Read an entire book of the Bible.

- Build a craft or project related to your Devotional Activity.

3. Disciplines Activities

Complete all three (3) of the following activities with your parent(s) as well as your Trail Guides and/or Troop Chaplain:

- Memorize and recite at least three (3) new Scripture verses, prayers, hymns, creeds, and/or catechisms discussed during the Devotional Activity.
- Maintain and pray over a prayer list on a daily basis for an agreed period of time.
- Regularly attend church services or mass for at least two (2) months.

4. Demonstration Activities

Complete both of the following activities with your Trail Guides and/or Troop Chaplain:

- Recite for your patrol and/or Trail Guides the three memory passages from the Disciplines Activities.

- Hold a final conference explaining what you have experienced and learned through the Worthy Life Award.

Woodlands Trail Mountain Lion

To achieve the Woodlands Trail Mountain Lion Worthy Life Award, you must complete the requirements in all four areas below with your parent(s) as well as your Trail Guides and/or Troop Chaplain as an active Trail Life USA Mountain Lion:

1. A Devotional Activity
2. A Discipleship Activity
3. Disciplines Activities
4. Demonstration Activities

The Devotional and Discipleship Activities are where Trailmen will choose, learn, and explore biblical principles. The Disciplines Activities are where the Trailmen apply their new knowledge to their lives. The Demonstration Activity is where the Trailman reports on his experiences to his peers and leaders. These activities may overlap with each other and should be integrated together when possible. Ensure that all completion dates are correctly documented in the Woodlands Trail Handbook and on www.TrailLifeConnect.com.

1. Devotional Activity

Participate in one (1) of the following activities with your parent(s) as well as your Trail Guides and/or Troop Chaplain:

An age-appropriate Bible study program consisting of at least ten (10) 30-minute sessions. Topics should focus on slightly advanced knowledge and skills of the Christian life, such as core doctrines, parables, obstacles to faith, biblical character studies, biblical manhood, Christian Worldview, spiritual disciplines, as well as the Trail Life program emphases of leadership, teamwork, character, wisdom, heritage, and faith.

Four (4) additional Values Branch Elective Steps.

2. Discipleship Activities

Participate in two (2) of the following activities and discuss them with your parent(s) as well as your Trail Guides and/or Troop Chaplain:

- Plan with others and participate in a community service project.
- Participate in a weekend mission trip or Christian retreat.
- Read three (3) entire books of the Bible.

3. Disciplines Activities

Complete all three (3) of the following activities with your parent(s) as well as your Trail Guides and/or Troop Chaplain:

- Memorize and recite at least three (3) new Scripture verses, prayers, hymns, creeds, and/or catechisms discussed during the Devotional Activity.
- Maintain and pray over a prayer list on a daily basis for an agreed period of time, track answers to prayers, and invite one other person to pray with you for your list.
- Regularly attend church services or mass for at least three (3) months.

4. Demonstration Activities

Complete both of the following activities with your Trail Guides and/or Troop Chaplain:

- Recite for your patrol and/or Trail Guide the three memory passages from the Disciplines Activities.
- Hold a final conference explaining what you have experienced and learned through the Worthy Life Award.

Navigators

To achieve the Navigators Worthy Life Award, you must complete the requirements in all four areas below with your parent(s) as well as your Trail Guides and/or Troop Chaplain as an active Trail Life USA Navigator:

1. A Devotional Activity
2. A Discipleship Activity
3. Disciplines Activities
4. Demonstration Activities

Ensure that all signatures and dates are correctly documented in the Trailman's Handbook and on TrailLifeConnect.com.

Work with your Trailmaster, Troop Chaplain, and mentor (approved by your parent or guardian) to create and document in your Handbook measurable goals, tasks, and reporting expectations before beginning any requirement. The Trailmaster, Troop Chaplain, and mentor must pre-approve, sign for completion, and date each activity. *Two-deep, No one-on-one, and Buddy system of Three* Youth Protection guidelines must be followed at all meetings with your mentor or leader(s).

1. Devotional Activity

Complete one (1) of the following activities and discuss it with your mentor:

- An age-appropriate Bible study program consisting of at least ten (10) one-hour sessions.
- One (1) Elective Trail Badge from the Values Frontier

- At least three (3) modules of the Manhood Journey program with your father or other male mentor.

2. Discipleship Activity

Complete one (1) of the following activities and discuss it with your mentor:

- Read a Christian book.
- Participate in a Christian weekend retreat or mission trip.
- Complete a service project using the Biblical principles or skills developed during your Devotional Activity.

3. Disciplines Activities

Complete three (3) of the following activities throughout your Devotional and Discipleship Activities:

- Keep a journal of questions, principles, and thoughts.
- Memorize and recite scriptures, prayers, hymns, creeds, or catechisms.
- Keep a prayer journal.

- Regularly attend services/mass at your local church.
- Volunteer to serve with your local church/parish on an ongoing basis.

4. Demonstration Activity

Complete a final conference with your Trailmaster, Troop Chaplain, and mentor, explaining what you have experienced and learned and how you have achieved your pre-determined goals, tasks, and expectations.

Adventurers

To achieve the Adventurers Worthy Life Award, you must complete the requirements in all four areas below with your parent(s) as well as your Trail Guides and/or Troop Chaplain as an active Trail Life USA Adventurer:

1. A Devotional Activity
2. A Discipleship Activity
3. Disciplines Activities
4. Demonstration Activities

Ensure that all signatures and dates are correctly documented in the Trailman's Handbook and on TrailLifeConnect.com. Work or activities undertaken for the Worthy Life Award cannot count toward any other program requirements (e.g. Horizon Award badges, Freedom Experiences, Servant Leadership Project, etc.) and vice versa.

Work with your Adventurer Advisor, Troop Chaplain, and mentor (approved by your parent or guardian) to create and document in your Handbook measurable goals, tasks, and reporting expectations before beginning any requirement. The Adventurer Advisor, Troop Chaplain, and mentor must pre-approve, sign for completion, and date each activity. *Two-deep, No one-on-one, and Buddy System of Three* Youth Protection guidelines must be followed at all meetings with your mentor or leader(s).

1. Devotional Activity

Complete one (1) of the following activities and discuss it with your mentor:

- An age-appropriate Bible study program consisting of at least twelve (12) one-hour sessions.
- The Band of Brothers Group Bible Study/Discipleship Program with a minimum duration of three (3) months.

2. Discipleship Activity

Complete one (1) of the following activities and discuss it with your mentor:

- Read a Christian book.
- Participate in a Christian weekend retreat or mission trip.
- Complete a service project using the Biblical principles or skills developed during your Devotional Activity.

3. Disciplines Activities

Complete three (3) of the following activities during your Devotional and Discipleship Activities:

- Keep a Bible study journal of questions, principles, and thoughts.
- Memorize and recite scriptures, prayers, hymns, creeds, or catechisms.
- Keep a prayer journal, including answers to prayers.
- Regularly attend services/mass at your local church.
- Volunteer to serve with your local church/parish on an ongoing basis.
- Share/explain the Gospel to at least ten people individually.

4. Demonstration Activities

Complete all three (3) of the following activities:

- Publicly share your personal testimony or Christian walk with your Troop or Bible study group.
- Make a significant presentation to your Troop or Patrol including important concepts learned during your activities.
- Hold a final conference with your Adventurer Advisor, Troop Chaplain, and mentor, explaining what you have experienced and learned and how you have achieved your pre-determined goals, tasks, and expectations.

Band of Brothers Bible Study and Discipleship Program

The purpose of the Band of Brothers is to provide the structure for a Christian group Bible study and discipleship program that is satisfactory for completing the Bible Study requirement of the Adventurers Worthy Life Award and aimed at building young men spiritually through Bible study and faith mentorship. The Band of Brothers program has young men disciple other young men in Christian growth under the advisement of adult mentor(s). Mentors must be Christian adults who have signed the Trail Life Statement of Faith and Values. Activities must be completed in conformity with Youth Protection Guidelines.

Youth Participation Requirements

All youth must be professing Christians. This program is specifically for Christian young men that have a special heart for Jesus and a desire to take their walk to a higher level of Christian growth and discipleship. Youth participants must be approved by the Troopmaster and Adventurers Advisor.

Group Structure

- Each group should develop a list of "ground rules" to guide the group's discussions and conduct.
- Groups should meet at least twice monthly during the school year for approximately 90 minutes per meeting.
- Each group may include Trailmen from any Troops within an Area.
- The group meets outside of normal Troop meeting times.
- Groups should be small enough in size (6-10) for everyone to participate.

Programming

- Each group selects their own discussion topics and meeting format. One suggested format is a small group Bible study with a youth leader fostering discussion and dialogue.
- Each group, with adult advisement, will periodically determine their focus of study (a Christian book, a book of the Bible, topic or

personality study from the Bible, a Bible study guide, etc.).

- Provide a social time at the beginning of each meeting.
- Provide meaningful corporate discussion time surrounding the study selected by the group.
- During meetings, groups may break up into smaller groups as accountability partners.
- Groups may plan additional events including fun, service, and spiritual with Mentor and Advisor approval.

Manhood Journey

Manhood Journey is a middle school program for grades 6 to 8. The purpose of the program is to provide a Christian discipleship program for our Troops that is aimed at building young men spiritually through Bible study and faith mentorship. As an introductory experience in discipleship, the Manhood Journey requires no formal training in ministry. The curriculum will guide the group along a trail of Bible study and discipleship. While the programming is intended for fathers and their sons, other adults who play a trusted role in a boy's life may and are encouraged to participate in lieu of a boy's father if necessary.

Leadership Requirements

Leaders must be Trail Life registered Christian adult leaders. Adult leaders must be approved by the Troop Committee or the Troop Ministry Liaison of the hosting Troop.

Other Parent / Adult Participation Requirements

Every effort should be made to include the boy participating with his father. The program allows them to grow together spiritually. Yet in any event, each boy should be accompanied by a father, male guardian, or a male adult leader.

Any non-related male mentor must be a registered member of Trail Life, having completed the appropriate background checks and Child Safety and Youth Protection Training.

If the father is not available, and in keeping with the "no one-on-one" protection policy, it would be advantageous to have two boys working with an adult leader. Under no circumstances shall an adult male be alone with a youth that is not his son. That includes driving to and from Manhood Journey meetings. This rule is sacrosanct and cannot be violated.

It is the responsibility of all involved, including the Charter Organization, the Troop Leadership, and the Manhood Journey participants to ensure that youth protection safeguards are in place.

Youth Participation Requirements

All youth are welcome to participate regardless of a profession of faith. However, a participating youth must be an active member of Trail Life.

Meeting Structure

- The format of conducting a meeting is entirely up to each group's preferences. It is suggested that a typical small group Bible study bye used, with a leader prompting the group with questions and guiding the group through its discussions. The goal is to foster discussion and dialogue, not a lecture by the adult leaders.
- At the inception of each group, the group should develop and agree upon a list of "ground rules" that will guide the group's discussions and conduct.
- Groups of no more than 15 are encouraged.
- Groups should meet at least bi-weekly.
- Each group may include boys and adults from a single Troop or multiple Troops within an area.
- It is recommended that the group meets outside of normal Troop meeting times so as not to draw

from normal Troop advancement or activity. Some Troops have scheduled overnight meetings at the church, weekend intensives, etc. in order to offer the Manhood Journey as a fun event.

- Each meeting will last at least an hour but could often go longer depending upon the topic and discussion, so plan accordingly.

Programming

The Manhood Journey is a third-party developed ministry. It already has a complete set of robust curricula available.

The Manhood Journey team has been extremely gracious in offering Trail Life members 4 immediate downloads as well as all 7 modules of their program absolutely **FREE**. These resources are available online at http://info.manhoodjourney.org/traillife using the following Coupon Code at checkout:

trail-life-module-coupon

More information on the program can be found on the main Manhood Journey website at

www.ManhoodJourney.org.

Length of Programming

The entire Manhood Journey is a two-year experience, with each module intended to contain six weeks of material. If a group were to meet bi-weekly, that's a full 72 weeks of content. That would include meeting year-round, not including the summer. The pace of completion is completely up to each group's discretion, with the goal of completing three modules in a year.

Also keep in mind that each module includes opportunities for service projects and faith experiences.

Be sure to plan your time accordingly so that your group takes advantage of these opportunities for Christian growth and mentorship.

Biblical Nature Quotes

Psalm 19:1 - The heavens declare the glory of God; the skies proclaim the work of his hands.

Romans 1:20 - For since the creation of the world God's invisible qualities—his eternal power and divine nature—have been clearly seen, being understood from what has been made, so that people are without excuse.

Psalm 104:24-25 - How many are your works, LORD! In wisdom you made them all; the earth is full of your creatures. There is the sea, vast and spacious, teeming with creatures beyond number— living things both large and small.

Job 12:7-10 - "But ask the animals, and they will teach you, or the birds in the sky, and they will tell you; or speak to the earth, and it will teach you, or let the fish in the sea inform you. Which of all these does not know that the hand of the LORD has done this? In his hand is the life of every creature and the breath of all mankind.

Psalm 96:11-12 - Let the heavens rejoice, let the earth be glad; let the sea resound, and all that is in it. Let the fields be jubilant, and everything in them; let all the trees of the forest sing for joy.

Psalm 50:10-11 - "For every beast of the forest is mine, the cattle on a thousand hills. I know all the birds of the hills, and all that moves in the field is mine."

Isaiah 11:6-9 - The wolf will live with the lamb, the leopard will lie down with the goat, the calf and the lion and the yearling together; and a little child will lead them. The cow will feed with the bear, their young will lie down together, and the lion will eat straw like the ox. The infant will play near the cobra's den, and the young child will put its hand into the viper's nest. They will neither harm nor destroy on all my holy mountain, for the earth will be filled with the knowledge of the LORD as the waters cover the sea.

Other Nature Quotes

Rachel Carson - "Those who contemplate the beauty of the earth find reserves of strength that will endure as long as life lasts."

Aristotle - "In all things of nature there is something of the marvelous."

Laura Ingalls Wilder - “If you truly love nature, you will find beauty everywhere.”

Hans Christian Andersen - "Just living is not enough. One must have sunshine, freedom, and a little flower."

John Muir - "In every walk with nature one receives far more than he seeks."

William Shakespeare - "One touch of nature makes the whole world kin."

John Muir - The clearest way into the Universe is through a forest wilderness.

Henry David Thoreau - I took a walk in the woods and came out taller than the trees.

Rachel Carson - There is something infinitely healing in the repeated refrains of nature – the assurance that dawn comes after night, and spring after winter.

William Shakespeare - The earth has music for those who listen.

Our Christian Worldview

Christianity is not a ***philosophy*** that explains things, it is a ***directive*** that shapes things. God lives outside of time and popular culture. He makes changes, change does not make him. Trail Life's Christian Worldview Principles are six statements on Truth, Creation, Human Dignity, Family, Stewardship, and Providence.

Truth

- There are absolute and unchanging truths about God and life.
- Morality and moral law are absolute and unchanging because they proceed from and reflect God's unchanging nature and character.
- A Trailman should show respect, understanding, and charity to others different from him, while maintaining firm Christian convictions.

Creation

- The eternal God created the universe for His purposes and according to His plan which is evident by the design, order and complexity of creation.

- All of God's creation is good. The entrance of sin into the world has affected every part of creation such that it is now fallen and imperfect.
- Because man is sinful and imperfect, he needs salvation through Jesus Christ alone.

Human Dignity

- Out of all God's creation, human beings are uniquely made in His image and likeness, and therefore all human life, from conception through natural death, has unquestionable value, worth, and dignity.
- Because each person is sacred and has intrinsic value, worth, and dignity, they should receive proper respect and protection, regardless of age, disability, economic status, ethnicity, location, race, sex or sinful tendencies.

Family

- By His design, God created men and women different from each other and uniquely for His purposes.
- God's design for marriage and family is that one man and one woman be united in marriage, and from that union the blessing of new life comes forth.
- Natural marriage which unites one man and one woman before God is an earthly reflection of God's Triune nature. Marriage also depicts the loving relationship between Christ and His church.

Stewardship

- God has given all human beings dominion over His earth and commanded us to use its natural resources.
- Therefore, each human being must be a good steward of the resources God provides and responsibly cultivate and conserve them for His glory.

Providence

- God is sovereign over all of history.
- God actively intervenes in peoples' lives for His purposes. He mysteriously uses all things—good and bad—for His glory.
- God is good and can be trusted in all things.

CPSIA information can be obtained
at www.ICGtesting.com
Printed in the USA
LVHW080624250620
658942LV00020B/2234

9 781951 472443